Praise for *Time Capsule*

"I have admired Nancy Gordon's clear-eyed and wise writing for years now. Her first collection, *Time Capsule,* is nothing less than a cause for celebration—each poem proof of a writer coming into her own, mining personal history and relationships for insights that appear so rarely in American poetry these days. Examining both love and mortality, these joyful poems 'celebrate our motley tunes,' and honor a life well-lived with wide-open eyes and heart."

—James Crews, author of *Love Is for All of Us, Unlocking the Heart,* and *Turning Toward Grief*

"Alongside its wisdom and joys, Nancy Gordon's *Time Capsule* seeks to contain the pain and losses that come with a long life: 'So many dances / trace their steps in my memory.' Whether speaking as Icarus or the Last Duchess, God or Eve, in sonnet or villanelle, on the ski slopes or dance floor or golf course, Gordon swings us from pathos ('As the oceans rise, / my eyes are also filling') to wry humor ('If music be the food of love, I'm hungry'). In poems that combine the 'bright intelligence' Gordon reads in a rescue dog's eyes with the 'cordial rhythm' she seeks in a lover, it's clear that 'her life and loves' have not 'finished blazing.'"

—Rebecca Starks, author of *Time Is Always Now*

"Nancy Gordon's *Time Capsule* is a potent meditation on love and loss, mixing memory with wit and a touch of humor. These poems share kinship with Elizabeth Bishop—spare and resonant, finely crafted, moving from sonnet to villanelle and back. Here is a poet who dreams in iambic pentameter, dances in her living room, grieves the burning planet, and revels in the clean cool air of an Adirondack morning. Amidst life's relentless changes, *Time Capsule* insists that music and poetry are a pathway to joy. Read it and be delighted."

—Diana Whitney, author of *Dark Beds*

Time Capsule

Time Capsule: Poems ©2025

Release Date: October 14, 2025

All Rights Reserved.
Printed in the USA.

Paperback ISBN: 978-1-57869-209-5

Library of Congress Control Number: 2025913292

Published by Rootstock Publishing
an imprint of Ziggy Media, LLC
Montpelier, VT 05602

info@rootstockpublishing.com
www.rootstockpublishing.com

Book design by Eddie Vincent, ENC Graphic Services.

Book cover photograph "Heart-Shaped red tree reflected in Fly Pond in the Adirondack Mountains of New York" by Colin D. Young, Shutterstock.com.

Author photo by Howard Gordon.

No AI training; no part of this book may be reproduced or transmitted in any form or by any means, electronic or mechanical, including photocopying, recording, or by an information storage and retrieval system (except by a journalist or reviewer who may quote brief passages in an academic or editorial review) without permission in writing.

For reprint permissions, or to schedule a book club visit or author reading, contact Nancy at npg.alt2@gmail.com.

Time Capsule

poems

by
Nancy Gordon

Montpelier, VT

For Howard, my husband and best friend for almost half a century, who encouraged and provided unending tech support for this chapbook.

Contents

First Tracks 1
Time Capsule 2
What Music Do We Hear? 4
Rescue Dog 5
Dogs Know 6
What Else Was Lost? 8
Autumn Blazes 9
For Mimi, ... 10
Caught by Words 11
Caught in a Line 12
I Envy the Amnesia of Buckets 13
Dear Heart 14
Ah, the Dance 16
This Year's Objective 18
Knowledge Worth Having 19
Calculations 20
Birdsong 21
Eve Ponders 22
Lake Placid Fragment 24
Not the Last Duchess 25
Icarus 26
Mist Again 28
The Ultimate Artist Looks Down at His Creation 29
The Range of Losses 30
Old Friendship 32
Chaucer's Worldview 33
Sunday Drive 34
Some Off Notes 35
Watching for My Great Grands 36

Sonnet for Two 37
The Cost 38
Dealing with Death 39
Saying Goodbye 40

Notes 42
Acknowledgments 43
About the Author 44

First Tracks

It starts snowing hard
as we walk home
up our mile of hilly road.
Well below freezing, snow
swirling, collecting
on the macadam.

You look back and say,
"My footprints are making tracks!"
Your words spur my memory,
"Remember when we used to make
first tracks at Vail, off Chair 14?"

We've not skied in years,
but our footprints now
take us back to early mornings
curving through last night's snow,
weaving, dipping, flying! laughing,
conquering the mountain.

We look back again,
smiling at our tracks
made from walking
together in the storm,
arthritic knees and hips managing.
But first tracks, nonetheless.

Time Capsule

I.

For a seventeen-year-old football halfback
tapping his knuckles on his desk
just loud enough to be heard
but not expelled from his required English class,
forty minutes more is an endless time.

For his teacher, a classroom veteran,
trying to reach the twenty-five years
required for a state pension,
trying not to hear those taps,
it seems even longer.

For the quiet girl in the second row
who doesn't lead cheers or date football players
and finds reading as essential as breathing,
forty minutes fly too quickly,
the discussion barely begun.

II.

Emerging from the terminal concourse,
Relieved passengers search for family or friends,
business signs with their names,
directions to taxis and buses.

A young woman sights a young man waving
and they smile, laugh, rush to each other.
Their weaving hug is a slow dance
whose music makes others smile
while waiting for their own reunions.

An older woman walks slowly,
her cane tapping a somber rhythm.
Several sad-eyed people reach for her,
hold her in a group hug.
"I can't believe he's gone."
"Grandma, we'll take care of you."

III.

Is life as short or as long
as a high school class period?
As decades that disappear
into a solitary flight?

What Music Do We Hear?
after Wallace Stevens

With only one full afternoon
to explore the Chicago Art Institute
I looked for the Impressionists room
and, on my way to that array,
found Picasso's Old Guitarist.

Stunned, I could not leave him.
He filled my eyes
as Wallace Stevens filled my mind.

> *They said, 'You have a blue guitar,*
> *You do not play things as they are.*
> *The man replied. 'Things as they are*
> *are changed upon the blue guitar.'*

But the guitar was brown.
All else was blue—the man,
the setting, his arm reaching down.
I got no further that afternoon
than The Old Guitarist and his tune.

And I wondered, as I looked and listened,
spellbound, if we ever know how things are
except as they're played on our own guitars,
in whatever colors we choose and play
to celebrate our motley tunes.

Rescue Dog

Jake comes into sight—ten pounds
of whirling golden fur, legs and feet a blur,
released from his leash to greet me,
racing toward me.
Eyes dark pools, shining, ears flapping
with his running and jumping—
up into my arms, onto my shoulder,
his body close to my chest—my heart.
Tongue lapping everywhere—"doggy kisses,"
says my friend who lets me share walks with him.
Quick breaths, his heart pounding, his body
warm and flexible as a gymnast's.

He drinks water from my hands.
He walks us. He explores the scents, the grass,
all that he can reach from his reattached leash.
He and my friend debate the boundaries.

When I have to leave, I turn to watch them go.
And Jake turns, looks back, looks back again,
crooks his head—
where are you going? aren't you coming with us?

Dogs Know

A dog knows if you like dogs.
If he interrupts walking
and sniffing the news
to consider you, he'll have
a good sense of whether it's worth
stopping to say hello.

Is it those eyes that decide, dark pools
with bright intelligence glowing,
making contact? Or his keen nose,
sensing a lack of fear or fight?

Is it the tone of your voice saying
Hello, oh good dog, you handsome thing
your hand out, palm down, back of hand
waiting, keeping still, for that exploratory
sniff, the touch—ah, the tongue.

A dog knows if you're a danger
to him—or worse, to the
person he's walking.

I was asked out on my first real date
by a handsome senior with a smooth line.
Just a thirteen-year-old sophomore,
I'd had a crush on him since the senior play.

A Saturday night date in our small town
meant the movies, and as the cool kids knew,
included necking in the back row
of the Hollywood Theater. Which wasn't yet
one of my activities.

My mother, still stunned by
my announcement that I had a date,
was already fretting. She worried more
when our dog growled as my new boyfriend
came in the door
to walk me to the movies.

Smart dog.

What Else Was Lost?

My brother and I long gone when it burned,
my mother long remarried and living in town.
The farmhouse rented out to others.
A generator in the shed
sparked the hundred-fifty-year-old wood.

Eight summers, several winters in that house
because the rent was low four miles out of town.
No phone, no electricity, dirt road,
water from a spring, when it didn't run dry.
I could trim the wick of a kerosene lamp,
and take a bath in a teakettle's worth of hot water.

My ice hockey stick must have been in the attic
when I left for college and the world.
The stick was wooden, slick, begged for at age ten,
after the boys let me play hockey one winter day
on the town's iced-over field behind the tennis courts.
I was going to play hockey forever.

Never used it. Was never asked to play again.
But I kept it. It moved with us, each year,
back to the farm for the summer, unused,
back into town for that winter's apartment,
till high school offered other diversions.

But I mourn that hockey stick.
Not as I mourn my skis,
which still felt like flying in my sixties,
or my rollerblades, donated about then
to a thrift shop when my orthopedist got fierce.

What other dreams burned in that farmhouse fire?

Autumn Blazes

Our northern autumn trees,
nourished by summer,
blaze briefly,
bursting with flames
of red, gold, orange,
a breathtaking bonfire
filling the mountainscape.

After rain and wind,
suddenly they're naked.
Their trunks look cold.
Their boughs are quiet.

Will I feel cold
like our trees?
Will there be silence
when I am naked,
when my life and loves
have finished blazing?

For Mimi,

who took in my brother and me (aged six and two)
when our mother's life imploded.

In the morning, you are at your desk in Chestertown
in the front corner of our small sunny living room,
smiling at me as I wake in my crib.
Your smile, in that sun, my earliest memory.

At night, you are the town's telephone operator,
up the long street and around the corner,
and when I pick the phone up in darkness
to tell you I'm going to the bathroom
your smiling voice says, "That's fine, dear."
I hear you again when I pick the phone up to say
I'm on my way back to bed.

You and Auntie Hazel and I walk up the street,
up the hill to the center of town.
You both break off pieces of the aloe plant
to treat some hurt on your hands.

When I turn around halfway there and raise my arms,
you always pick me up.
And you smile like the sun, warming me always.

Caught by Words

The ten-year-old girl loved to read.
Comic books, movie mags, cereal boxes.
It wasn't just love, but a need.
Printed words were a powerful magnet.

While looking for something to read
She found a book of her brother's
and was happily reading *The Sheik,*
unaware it was risqué to others.

Big brother then faked some concern
for his young sister's moral decay
and her mother demanded return
and a promise she had to obey.

So she promised she would not complete it.
Then found the book easily next day
read the rest, after skipping a chapter,
so could keep her word in a way.

Big brother, the hero, was praised,
their mother impressed with his caring.
The girl had a touch of malaise
but was cheered by her own kind of daring.

Caught in a Line

"We were talking about iambic pentameter,"

said I in my strange dream, trying for composure,
to the woman who found her husband
lying next to me, in my dream,
where we were discussing poetry.

Said the teacher, trying for control,
to the students
as they talked, texted, laughed,
learned other rhythms.

Said the poet, trying to convey magic,
to her listeners, wanting all
to feel those sounds, those images.

Say I to you, trying for calm,
as my hand insists on reaching
for your face.

I Envy the Amnesia of Buckets

What would I like to forget?
You might know, but
you're not here to ask.

Well, not air
or snow
or Adirondack woods.

Not ice cream
or hot dogs
or early morning coffee.

Not the rush of skiing
the therapy of walking
the steely click of a
golf ball well struck.

Not the lines of poems
or the words and worlds
of books.

But. Maybe... you.

I am working on forgetting
how you felt.
Your skin. I mean, your body.
Your eyes, smiling,
blessing my closeness.

Maybe I'll forget
others I have loved and lost,
who were not mine
to keep.
But. Not you. Not yet.

Dear Heart

You play so many roles.
You literally pump blood
(I thank you for long and active service.)

Your imagined red shape serves
as a charitable or holiday symbol,
especially in February.

You hold secrets, love, compassion,
even some residual hatred
for cruelties to those I love.

You are the center of the matter,
whatever that matter might be,
perhaps a legal dispute.

People urge
others to "take" you,
for courage or encouragement,
for consolation.

Your chambers hold life, hold love.
A friend says, "I hold you in my heart."
Do you have hands?

How much room do you have, Heart?
Are you really "as boundless as the sea,
as infinite," as Juliet proclaimed?

Is there a sound when you are broken?
Maybe a snap? A loud crack?
Or perhaps a slow exhaling

of all that air of hope and joy
as if a balloon were deflating
after someone you had held close
slipped out the back window?

I'll tell you a secret, Heart.
The last time someone broke you,
I didn't hear you snap or exhale.

There was only silence.
Except for my crying.

Ah, the Dance

> "The feet remember the dance..."
> —Joyce Sutphen, "What the Heart Cannot Forget"

High school dances
in the gym.
Square dances, slow dances,
Charleston revival (watch my knees!)
Polkas to spin the building around.

At 17, the rumba at the local night spot
with my friend's big brother,
love of my heart for years,
two months before his wedding.
I dressed in black jersey, clingy,
wanting to show him
what he was missing
by not waiting for me to grow up.

In my twenties, the samba
at the senior prom
for the high school kids I taught.
I showed up just late enough
so they were seated and watching
as we danced our entrance
across the ballroom floor,
my drama teacher colleague
and I, dressed in black again, but
a cocktail dress this time, not clingy
but crinkly and sparkling,
loving how the kids' jaws dropped.

In my thirties, the dance of our eyes,
lying with my handsome Brit
in the heather of Northern Scotland,

where we'd met.
Later I flew from New Jersey to London
to dance with him, but—married—
he stayed in step with his wife.

Then, as my mother cried
for my singleness as I approached forty
and my plan to save for retirement,
a handsome professor showed up
in a tweed jacket.

We made a permanent date
and for years we danced in the living room.
Paul Simon was going to Graceland, and we
joined the rhythm if not the direction,
synchronized, with the beat and the urgency,
twirling, moving away and back,
catching each other's hands.

In our sixties, at a cousin's wedding
in Houston, we expected to leave
the reception early.
We danced till the lights went out.
The relatives cheered.

Years later, my feet dance
whenever they hear music,
any kind of music, even commercials,
though the knees won't always
follow.

So many dances
trace their steps in my memory.

Won't you dance with me?

This Year's Objective

My goal for this recovery year is plain—
a day that passes with no thoughts of you.
The object is to discontinue pain.

I had some hope for what we might retain
but it was all much more than you could do.
My goal for this recovery year is plain.

What you started, you could not maintain.
I understand, your marriage wasn't through.
My object is to minimize my pain.

I hope for genuine calm I can sustain.
I'd like to know that I can say adieu.
My goal for this recovery year is plain.

With an air of casual distance to maintain
I'll try my best to keep on making do.
My object is to master losing pain.

No lingering thoughts, no grudges to retain,
fresh light for me and, yes, as well for you.
My hope for this recovery year is plain—
the object is to discontinue pain.

Knowledge Worth Having

My physics professor husband
did not know for quite a while
how to change a toilet paper roll,
where the paper towels are,
that we have gadgets to open jars
though I had used them in plain sight,
and once professed not to know
where the grocery store was
when we ran out of milk.

But he has always known
how to end an email with "Lubya."
And in the darkness,
after we've said goodnight
and turned out the light,
how to reach out with his hand
and hold mine for a moment.

Calculations

My husband is a physicist by trade.
He loves his numbers much as I love words.
Proudly he'll recite the totals made
by Pi, some trillions, as you've heard.

As his numbers leave me in the past
our syncopation rests on our good will.
And my words may confound him, whirling fast.
We listen, we make time, we do the drill.

Uh oh, I just read him what's above
and now I'm hearing trigonometry.
He thinks I'll understand, because I loved
trig years ago—it's now long lost to me.

Ancient scores do not yield current knowledge
and no way will I go back to college.

Birdsong

On a clear Adirondack morning
I wake early, stretch, open a big window.
The distant mountains and solid blue sky
fill my eyes, the clean cool air fills my lungs, my heart.

I hear the birds planning their day.
Their chirping swirls around our birches,
which stoop to welcome them
and ask how they can help.

Our fat pines stand aloof, unheeding.
I'm glad the birds ignore their needling.
The birds swoop in various groups,
filling our air space with chatter.

Would I plan my day with greater joy
if I could float and fly with friends in the sky
and sing as we negotiate directions?

Eve Ponders

There are all sorts of creatures here.
The one that looks the most like me
walks upright on two legs, as I do,
and has two arms, as I do, two hands
which let us grab or hold things.

He seems pleasant enough, but he's
not very interesting. He keeps talking
about names he thought of
 for what he calls birds and beasts.
He complains about pain in his side.

And he keeps coming toward me,
keeps touching my front. I'm not
sure how I feel about that.
Is he supposed to do what he does?
Well, yes, it's not so bad, but what's the point?

And what is there to do here, for me?
It's pretty stifling.
(I just made up that word.)
Everything is named, things grow,
what else is there to do?

Oh. Hi. I think he said your name is Serpent.
You're really skinny—and long
but it's fun talking with you,
and at least you offer me
tasty things to eat.

What, today, something called
an apple? Sure.
Ah, it's crisp, it's tart.
Oh my.
Hey, can you
get me the hell out of here?

Lake Placid Fragment

Cold gray Adirondack day.
Groups of tourists wander
up and down Main Street,
stout couples, children trailing,
dressed in hopeful shorts, action tee shirts.
They stare at store fronts,
see their gray reflections,
enter stores, walk out again.
Looking for lunch menus.
Trying to find their vacation days.

Not the Last Duchess

Look at you standing there!
Bragging to the Count's emissary
about my portrait. Proud
of its beauty, hinting
at its value.

Stupid sot.
Cruelest of masters.

You keep this remnant of me
locked in this room, like money.

Well, my Duke, hear yet another message
from the honorable Count, engaged by you
to seek and send a pliant, willing
(and virginal) young thing
to be your next Duchess.

You, my Duke,
will be sent a pretty face, a silly girl.
But not the Count's daughter, though
you think she's all but bargained for,
because—some news, my love—
the Count knew me rather well
and was not pleased with what
he learned of your ineptness, your heartless
ownership, your haughty, ugly self.

My dear Count caused me more smiles,
more flushes of joy,
than ever you could, my Lord.

Icarus

Hey, Ozzy, buddy!
What are you doing?
Trying to fly high,
going after that cheerleader blonde?

You jerk.
You think that'll work?

You get too close to that classy chick,
and you're dirt.
Or in the dirt, face down.

Remember that dumb poem
Miss H made us read?
Some English dude
talking about a painting by a guy
whose name I couldn't pronounce?

A kid flew too close to the sun,
and his damn wings melted.
For all that showing off,
then crashing—
damn, nobody even noticed.

Come on, Oz,
don't aim so high,
It's too much stress.
Try for that pudgy girl in Bio
with the cute face.
She'll say yes.

Don't burn your wings, Oz,
it ain't worth it.
 Nobody has to know
where you wanted to go.

Mist Again

Morning fog blurs the world,
obscures the pines and maples
that line the fairway and
the distant curves of the golf course.

I hit my drive on the first hole
and the ball disappears.
For my second shot (hoping for par)
I find my ball behind a tree,
so it will take at least three
to get to the green,
a sure bogey in the mist.

How many shots have I missed
in the fog of life, whose mornings
may resemble this round of golf?
How many decisions have been
misdirected, obscured?

Perfection is elusive
in either game, but
even on a bad day
You keep trying
To hit some good shots.

The Ultimate Artist Looks Down at His Creation

You will have rain
on this summer solstice.
Today the palette is gray.
Grays in any shade will do.

I'll be watching
but don't expect help.
You've damaged the earth.
You've used up your colors.
You've spent your brightness.

But see if you can use gray
in all its permutations,
perhaps some acrylic turns
and splashes with palette knives,
some slashes that excite
and show some energy,
a few new and lighted paths.

See if you can use gray
to make a day worth my waiting
for your final display.

The Range of Losses

Many lost things can be replaced.
Car keys? Call the dealer.
House keys? Take your spare
to the hardware store, have them
cut extras. Credit card?
Call, cancel, get a new number.

But can lost friends be found again?
Some move away, too far
for lunch or a short walk together.
Distance increases, real or created.
Emails get shorter, stop coming.
Sometimes silence follows an angry word.
Time passes.

After too many busy years and lengthening silence,
I searched online for an old friend.

We met as camp counselors in the Adirondacks,
and took our afternoons off together
whenever we could, often canoeing
down the lake for lunch with mountain views
and endless talk and laughter.

I flew to be in her wedding in Ohio
visited her as her family grew in Oneonta,
listened to her life, cheered her leadership
of a summer opera festival.

When I finally searched, I wanted to say
before we got any older
how special she had been in my life,
how I remembered the fun we'd had
as camp counselors, how we'd laughed
and talked so easily for many years.

I found her obituary.

I've never cried for my keys.

Old Friendship

This morning I dropped a cereal bowl,
a gift from you years ago, gentle pottery glazed
with ocean and sky colors, wisps of clouds.

It shattered, leaving haphazard fragments.
Looking down, I wondered if this shard art
might be a metaphor for our friendship.

Beautiful but broken, by distance, and time,
anger, misunderstandings,
more and more fragments of silence.

I have no golden glue for repair.
I swept up the pieces.
The floor is clean.

Chaucer's Worldview

My professor once said
that Chaucer, surveying
his worlds, decided
he could either
laugh or cry
and chose to laugh.

Adopting that choice
has kept me afloat.
But politics, pandemics,
shootings, and storms
now threaten my comic view.
As the oceans rise,
my eyes are also filling.

Sunday Drive

If music be the food of love, I'm hungry.
Let's drive, how about our favorite wooded place
but I need some song to tune the mood.
We'll harmonize with sound as well as touch.

Maybe some of that 1970s nostalgia
or let's hear Leonard's "Hallelujah"!
Just the tone for our romantic romp.
But what? No music here?

I thought you had the newest, topline car.
No CD drive? They're outdated? No!?
Here in my hands I have the perfect tracks
to nourish our terrific timeout fling.

Turn around, it's not going to work.
No music means no dancing. Sorry, friend.

Some Off Notes

We didn't make enough
euphony together, you say
with a smile suggesting
I'm the one
who played off key.

I've heard you say
to mutual listeners
that my sound is
cacophony—not
mellifluous or mellow,
but discordant, dissonant,
as disconnected as you
and I seem to be.

I miss our emotional harmony.
We made good music together
till you started hitting
the wrong notes on purpose,
telling me you needed
to get an octave higher.

Hope your solos
are sounding good.
Me, I'm sitting here
pounding the keys
blowing the notes
till someone comes along
with a more cordial rhythm.

Watching for My Great Grands

The Canadian fires blew smoke last year,
shrouding our northern mountains.

Haters of learning ban books,
shrouding paths to understanding.

Can the fires be contained?
Can written wisdom be maintained?

As more crusaders challenge climate change
and shout distortion of our histories,
our humanness is fading away.

Oh, children, beautiful little ones,
I can hardly see you
through this haze, this maze.

Sonnet for Two

Our lives are now a failing masquerade.
I've tired of our posturing for show.
We've lied too much, in making this charade.
I'm leaving, thought I'd better let you know.
We've done our best to keep things looking right.
You'd hug me when we partied, take my hand.
That we could barely manage not to fight
our friends most likely failed to understand.
So, let's just call this awkward aging game
before the next round devastates us both.
Hang on—no blaming here, it's just a shame
that neither you nor I could keep our faith.
And yet—are we too close to pull apart?
Confession here—I hold you in my heart.

The Cost

My body ages, and my mind; the mirror shocks, a new acquaintance.
Will it take a loss of memory to acquire acceptance?

My mother fought, then yielded, to forgetfulness.
Is stillness, the ease of such rest, the price of acceptance?

I walk up and down paths, around lakes. I swing golf clubs.
I bicycle new roads, their smoothness offering acceptance.

Dorian Gray's portrait showed him still young, beautiful, but when
he stabbed it, he fell—dead, loathsome, decrepit— no acceptance.

Oh, lovers in my past, would you recognize my sagging body,
still touch me so generously? I work on acceptance.

The aging rescue dog, new to me, is cautious, advances, retreats,
comes closer, reaches to lick my hand, his token of acceptance.

Dealing with Death

Greetings, dark hunter,
is it time for another game?
What round are we on?

Have you placed your Ace of Spades?
Who shuffles the deck today?
Is it still your turn to deal?

You don't frighten me with your fiendish smile
your guile in finding me more quickly,
looming nearer to your prey each day.

Well, I'm getting closer to welcoming your
inevitable win, but the game is still fun
for more rounds, at least one.

So—till I fade some more and forget
the good hands I've held,
don't deal that death card quite yet.

Saying Goodbye

So you come up to me and say
Geez, I kinda love you, and
if I could do somethin about it,
I would, but I can't.
Then I say, Geez, that's really somethin,
I guess I kinda love you, yeah,
But I can't do anythin about it.
I'm kinda committed.

We'll still be friends, you say, but first
I kinda wanna hold your hand
and have a little kiss,
before we're just friends again.
And I say, yeah,
I'd kinda like to see how that feels.
And we have a hug or two.

And it feels good,
and we aren't gettin around
to the bein just friends part.
And I say, Geez
what is this? Are we on
some kinda farewell tour?

And you say,

Don't knock it, great idea.
Cher kept puttin em on
and pullin em off,

kept em going for years.

Notes

Ah the Dance: "The feet remember the dance . . ." This line is from Joyce Sutphen's poem, "What the Heart Cannot Forget" in *Coming Back to the Body* (Holy Cow! Press, 2000).

I Envy the Amnesia of Buckets: This title is a line from Jane Hirshfield's poem, "A Bucket Forgets Its Water" in *Ledger* (Alfred A. Knopf, 2020).

What Music Do We Hear: includes lines from Wallace Stevens' poem "The Man with the Blue Guitar" in *The Man with the Blue Guitar & Other Poems* (Alfred A. Knopf, 1937).

Saying Goodbye is the winner of the Mary Margaret Audette Memorial Award from the Poetry Society of Vermont, judged by Geof Hewitt, and will be published in the 2026 edition of *The Mountain Troubadour*.

Acknowledgments

Thank you to poet and lifetime friend Alice Wolf Gilborn for suggesting a few years ago that I try a poetry workshop.

Thank you to James Crews and to Rebecca Starks, each of whom led workshops that challenged, encouraged, and inspired those of us who had the good fortune to participate in them.

Thank you to the Saturday Poets, Shari Altman, Alice Wolf Gilborn, Mary ("Ray") Goehring, and Susan Zimmerman, for our weekly meetings for the last five years where we write, share, and discuss poetry.

Thank you to Diana Whitney, poet and editor, for thoughtful editing and encouragement.

My gratitude to the editors of the following publications, where these poems originally appeared, sometimes in different forms:

Rescue Dog: The Path to Kindness, ed. James Crews, 2022.

I Envy the Amnesia of Buckets: Literary North's Constellation, 2021.

First Tracks: ZigZag's Chapbook No. Five, Otter Creek Poets, 2021.

Sonnet for Two and **What Music Do We Hear?**: *The Mountain Troubadour*, Poetry Society of Vermont, 2024.

About the Author

Nancy Gordon was born in New Brunswick, New Jersey in 1938, and grew up in two Adirondack small towns.

College summers spent as a camp counselor made her think of trying teaching as a career. Grateful for scholarship aid, she graduated from Wellesley College in 1958, and a fellowship from Wesleyan University's Master of Arts in Teaching program gave her the credentials required for teaching in public schools. She taught high school English and creative writing for most of the next seventeen years in two New Jersey high schools, which included teaching for a year in Auckland, New Zealand, on a Fulbright Hays exchange grant. During part of a sabbatical she studied in Oxford, in a program open to American graduate students. She still treasures her card for the Bodleian Library, where she swore "not to ignite flames therein" and was impressed that the ladies room graffiti was in Latin.

She met her husband when they were both visiting family in Northern New York and both went to a Christmas party that neither of them had planned to attend. Both north again that summer, they had a date, were engaged a month later, and were married on New Year's Day, 1976, in the Adirondacks. She moved to Miami, expecting to continue teaching, but opportunities were limited. She decided to go to law school and graduated magna cum laude from the University of Miami School of Law in 1982. She practiced law for thirty years, mostly as in-house counsel.

Retiring from law practice in 2012, she had more time for poetry, and found some poetry groups.

In 2020, a poet friend asked if she might be interested in a poetry workshop with James Crews. She joined that workshop, which was a substantial start to the poetry world as she now knows it. She did two more workshops with James and then started, with several other workshop attendees, a poetry group, the Saturday Poets, who have met weekly online, with occasional weeks off, ever since. James said they were the Saturday Poets that meet on Wednesday. One of her poems was published in Crews's 2022 anthology, *The Path to Kindness*.

In 2024, she joined the Poetry Society of Vermont, which published two of her poems in their 2024 *Mountain Troubadour* and awarded her two Honorable Mentions for poems submitted to the 2024 PSOV summer contests.

She and her husband currently live in Lake Placid, New York for more than two-thirds of the year. It's home.

🍃We Grow Our Books in Montpelier, Vermont

Learn more about our titles in Fiction, Nonfiction, Poetry and Children's Literature at the QR code below or visit www.rootstockpublishing.com.